*J*ust *P*eople

*and other poems
for young readers*

&

*P*aper/*P*en/*P*oem:
A Young Writer's Way to Begin

About the cover:
Good Things Come in Pears
We found the pear in a large supermarket bin full of different kinds, shapes, sizes and colors. This one seemed perfect. A perfect pear, also perfect as the illustration for the poem, "The Inner Ear." That too was a perfect pair.

When the heart and mind are also paired, as they were in the creation of this book, a kind of reverie occurs. That's what happened when our pair of editors chose the photograph of the pear for the cover. It was the perfect choice.

Not only does the pear invite us to listen to the poetry, it symbolizes the pairing that runs throughout the book:

    poet/photographer
    poems/photographs
    text/invitations
    author/reader
    paper/pen
    heart/heart

There are also many pairings within the poems themselves. Look for them. Find them. Take a bite and enjoy.

K.A & K.A.

Just People

and other poems
for young readers

&

Paper/Pen/Poem:
A Young Writer's Way to Begin

Poems
&
Invitations
by
Kathi **A**ppelt

Photographs by Kenneth Appelt

That is question now;
And then comes answer like an Absey book,
King John, i, 1
Shakespeare

Absey & Company
Houston, Texas

Dedicated to:
Jacob and Cooper
two people, beloved

Acknowledgements

Many people have walked beside me on my own writing way. To them I owe a tremendous debt of gratitude. In particular I want to thank my teachers Elizabeth Neeld, Venkatesh Kulkarni, Lou Kelly, Betty Unterberger and Paul Christensen.

This book could not have happened without the assistance of Marianne Windsor and Clarice Whiteker, both ninth-grade teachers at Lufkin Jr. High East--and their students, especially J.T., Aaron, and Michele.

I also want to thank my writing partners Donna Cooner, Debbie Leland, David Rosen, Jo Spiller, Anne Bustard, and Toni King, as well as the members of my journaling group.

This book would have remained only a dream without Edward Wilson, Joyce Armstrong Carroll, and Jerry James who have walked through it page by page, word by word, day by day, throughout the long year that it took to bring it to life.

And of course, my family. It's love that makes it all possible. Thank you.

Kathi

Contents

Just People

Paper/Pen/Poem: A Young Writer's Way to Begin

Just People

*and other poems
for young readers*

At the Carnival Last Night

They were
buckled up
in a blue and red cup
fastened tight
the two of them alone
not needing to say a thing
nothing
eyes on the ground
as bright as day
faces in the sky
as bright as night.
When the carny
pulled the brake,
they stopped
just below the planets
Jupiter Saturn Mars
where he kissed her.
Only the stars saw
(stars don't tell).
And it was "thank you Mr. Ferris"
all the way to Earth.

Who Would've Thought

Latoya Bentson's living room
was actually a launching pad?

It looked like any other living room:
    couch   lamp   LazyBoy
    coffee table   philodendron

'til last Friday night when
Latoya turned the music
s-o-o-o loud
her great great aunt in the picture frame
    rattle-rattle-rattled
s-o-o-o much
her mama grabbed that aunt
and   hurry-hurry-hurried
to the other side of the house
where it was not
s-o-o-o loud

but not me and not Latoya
and not Susie Myers
and not the Alexander twins
with their matching toes and frizzy hair

'cause the
      beat
            beat
                  beat
and our
      feet
            feet
                  feet

got all tangled up
beat, beat
    feet
feet, beat
'til *u-u-u-up* we went right off the floor!

Yes!

Good thing Latoya's house had a ceiling there
else who knows
    goodness knows!
where we might have gone

        spinning
    spinning   spinning
        spinning

through the
    living air
in Latoya Bentson's
    living room
last
    Friday
        night.

Fields

Alone on my grandmother's quilt
in the grassy field behind her house
cotton-thin
spun

I lie in a field of stars
sliver-thin
spinning.

The Airshow, c. 1929

nobody knew
the real reason
she walked on that wing: she
needed to hear
something else
something besides those folks on the tarmac
the ones she met in town every day

from her perch
she could see their mouths move up and down
spewing mean puffs of words toward her
    crazy fool
    out of her mind
    tramp
    did you see the way
    her dress clung to her like that
    you could see every curve
    her parents must be heartbroken
    course what kind of parents
    would let their girl do such a thing?

what they didn't know
what they never would—
how good it felt to leave them all behind
to hear only the rush of
wings

Tips from my Grandfather

"You hold it like this," he'd say,
the flat stone, same size as a silver dollar,
same brownish-gray as his hair,
rested atop the circle made by his
third finger and thumb, a nest.
"Loose, loose," he'd say. Then with a sideways
snap of his right arm and wrist, he'd send it
flying across the lake, a comet,
trailing its silver tail across the water,
until it burned through the surface
and disappeared forever.
"The secret is in the grip," he'd say,
"A stone can't skip if it's held too tight."

Lunch

After the divorce
my mother moved us
far away from our old familiar
neighborhood, our old familiar school.
"We need a fresh start," she said,
and packed all we owned
into our familiar Buick with its
blue vinyl seats.

The hardest part:
not the long journey across
the bayous to the other side of town
or my father's downcast face
when we pulled away.
It was eating lunch by myself.
The new school cafeteria
didn't serve fresh starts,
just old familiarities
to every one but me.

Swifts

Three swifts arrive
astonished to find me here,
alone on their veranda.
What do they discuss, I wonder,
when this place is empty?
Do they gather on the swing
just as we
and talk about what matters—

the way
the spider spun her web across the bell peppers,
how the barn cat
had her litter in the rim of the mower's tire?

Couldn't
    our words waft out
        catch the porch's breeze

            moths   free for the taking?

What's to keep the swifts
    from scooping them up?

    swallowed whole

What's to keep a prayer on the wing?

Emergence

My father's Ford was a cocoon that day

the only thing driving—
rain against the windshield
sliding down the glass
erasing the familiar terrain of the driveway.
Behind the steering wheel, alone,
too young to turn the key
but wanting to
oh yes, wanting to

beside me   a map
red circles wrapped around towns that beckoned:
    Magnolia, North Carolina
    Bloomsburg, Pennsylvania
    Garden City, Idaho
    Meadowbrook, Illinois
places spun together with blue threads
thin as silk

come, they whispered, *come . . .*

soon, it won't be long,
I'll send you a postcard from every stop I make

it's only a matter of waiting
for my folded wings to dry

Mutual Attraction

the cat needs the sun

   to electrify his fur

   recharge his motor

   make his eyes glow beneath the bed, red beams

   add steam to his hiss

   mark the birds' shadows

   give him night vision

the sun needs the cat —

   last true worshiper

A Pillow Case

I'll have to be patient, strong,
willing to stay for the long haul.
See, they don't even show up before the tenth hour
after midnight—
the big boss dreams,
the ones that come in colors—
greenblueorangeredyellowfuchsia.

Then I'll need at least another two hours
to get them straight, sort them out and all.
So, don't wake me up 'til noon this Saturday.
I can make the sacrifice.

Side by Side

The cemetery angels stood side by side
without their heads,
a mother and her babe.
I like to think they were
taken one night by a lost boy
who chipped away at them,
careful not to harm their shaded eyes
or graceful lips.
His was no vengeful beheading
or malicious act of violence.
No, he only wanted the
angels' heads for company
on dark nights when the wind swirled
around him, and after all he
couldn't carry their bodies
their heavy marble wings.
Besides, what he needed most were their quiet
expressions of peace beside him
while he slept. Then he felt not quite so lost.
Not quite so cold.

Could it be that if we
found the angels,
we might find the boy too?

The Swimmer

knows a moment
just beyond the place
where she thinks she can't go on
her chest aches
legs tighten
every muscle screams
a moment when
all at once
each stroke becomes a perfect prayer
and breathe
pull
breathe
pull
she glides through
the oh so thin boundary
between skin and water
water and sky
selkie and girl

it's when the water
gives her to the air
and asks only that she not forget.

Giving Up

The bike was too small for me
but if I gave it up
it would go to my younger sister
who wouldn't remember it was M. I. N. E.

so I kept it
even though my knees
bumped against the handlebars
calves cramped

"Don't you think you're too big for that bike?" Mother
    asked.
My sister stood beside her, nodding.

I stood up on the pedals
and coasted by
Never, I cried.
Mother pulled my sister's hair back behind her ears,
where it floated, blonde, above her shoulders.

That afternoon
the bike turned too sharp beneath me
and threw me hard against the asphalt.
Worse, it swung its bare handlebar
into my forehead and carved a perfect
circle between my eyes
a third eye.

Sight is the most powerful of the senses.

The Pebble

When he saw the pebble,
gleaming among pebbles,
my little son heard a Voice

    Take and eat.

And so he did,
pushed it into that
moist place between jaws
where no teeth sat.
The sparkling cold of it   bit his gum,
so he pressed it against
juicy flesh of his cheek
until all cold was sucked away.

Oh, how the salt sung to him.

And the Voice rang in: *Alleluia!*

Then he rolled it across
the roof of his mouth
exact center of the universe
his tongue's tip,
      tested shape,
             tasted worth.
At last it came to rest
against tiny front teeth   tap

There it sat,
Round, warm, perfect.

Remember? asked the Voice,
this is how the oyster makes a pearl.

Javier

Javier, he was so cold that day
only a thin t-shirt and old jeans
to keep the icy air
from rubbing his ribs raw
only thin rubber soles
between his feet
and the cold concrete
with still an hour before the
bell rang

Mrs. Rivera the librarian, she saw him
she couldn't look directly
at his blue lips
or his naked arms
without shivering
but Mrs. Rivera, she could break the rules and
let him in
led him into that warm room
with its burnished tables
flame-stitched chairs
toasted books

Javier, he had a quick notion of heaven
and when he found that book
someone left opened to a
page of mustangs
wild and shaggy
ears back   free
well Javier, he burned that page
into a place behind his sight
and kept it there all morning
all through the day
always

and now
when you see Javier
wild and shaggy
ears back free
look at that tall, proud boy
the icy air the cold concrete
lost their grip
Javier, he's been to heaven
mustangs are there.

That **K**iss

He couldn't explain at all
what it was like
that kiss
the one he gave
accidentally
to the girl on the stairs.
He hadn't meant to kiss her
except he did mean to
sometime
just not exactly then
on the way up the stairs
between history and English.
It was like it wasn't *him* who kissed her
even though he was
the one
then he couldn't explain
anything—
the feeling
the floating
the air rushing by.
All he knew was this:
sometime after the French Revolution
somewhere in the Universe
he found himself in English
before the bell rang
without taking a single step
after that kiss.

Tropism

You need:
a seed
dirt
water
Without a sound
Gravity pulls down
Light pulls up. . .

    Tug-of-war
in a paper cup.

Keeping His Head
For Jacob

People were always telling him:

> "Get your head out of the clouds!"

as if the clouds were a bad place for his head to be.
He liked having it there
where his thoughts could bump into each other
and even rain when they got too heavy.
He could think of worse places . . .
But in the day-to-day of things
it didn't work out to be so distant, so dreamy,

s o   s p a c e d   o u t.

His teachers and parents were
happier if he kept his head in mathematics
and current events. They didn't know
how hard it was, especially on clear days
when he could see the white shapes outside his win-
dow—

    Cumuli, nimbi, strati
             aye, aye, aye
                    it made him dizzy.

That's why he dyed his hair blue, you see:
to keep the sky nearby
while he was required to keep his head
                    on earth.

Sacred Bear of Hokkaido

Higuma wanders--
      to the mountainside's temple
winter carves a path.

The Inner Ear

Listen, the ear
    knows the bear groans when she sleeps
    swears the drummer missed his beat
    wears gold and nickel
    holds old rhymes for years and years
    is yearning's sister
    would learn your true name
    admires the pear's shape
    hopes shears won't slip
    fears it'll miss the telephone's ring
    makes a cup for tears

Where the Colors Slip Through

You know it's early
but go anyway.
Step softly into the barn
warm and still.
Serena rubs her forehead against your chest.
Sweet pony,
Give her oats, invite her, "Come with me.
It isn't far."

No need for a saddle,
Just a bridle.

Lead her into the damp air
settling on your cheek,
past the barn,
past the house
into the waking day.

Shh . . . walk quietly, the two of you.
the colors still sleep.

Now the world is wrapped in black and gray.
Soft.
Quiet.

Walk past the silent trees.
Even the night animals
have finished their rounds.
The owl—returned to her nest,
The wolf—done with her singing,
The rabbit—safe in his burrow.
This, their dream hour.

It's only you and your pony.
When you get to the stream
climb onto her back,
leave the reins loose
and rub her neck beneath her mane.
Don't hurry,
she knows the way.
She'll carry you across the meadow
where fog angels
dance above silver grass.
Watch them slip aside as you pass.
Look back,
they're holding hands.

And all you hear are Serena's steps—
steady.

When you reach the lake's edge
where stars still float,
you can't see
where water stops
and sky begins.

Serena finds the trail
to the top of the bluff.
You climb and climb,
it seems so far, and
even though the path
isn't steep
you hold tightly
Serena's mane.

When she stops
you're there.
At the top.

Slide down your pony's back.
and stand beside her
close to the edge,
close.
Below the valley waits,
like you.
And all around is blue,
deep blue.

You lean against Serena,
your cheek on her silky neck.

Soon, above the far hill
there comes a sharp sliver of light.
The colors!
all the greens and blues and browns,
the reds and purples and yellows—
slip through from the other side.
It's why you came.

Listen, the quiet's gone,
the dark far behind you,
Shh . . .
Don't say a word,
don't even whisper.

Simply
hold out your arms
and welcome
Dawn.

Just People

At Mirabeau B. Lamar High School
    there were plenty of heroes.

There was Jonathan Thomas—quarterback sensation
Ashley Riggerio—head cheerleader
Deanna Braden—Miss Teen Texas.
Sandy Hampton—whiz bang math genius.
The glamour crowd.

Certainly Marsha Cates—last chair French horn player
in the marching band—wasn't one of them.
And neither was her boyfriend Collie Simms—
    just an average student.
They went unnoticed by most, by teachers,
especially by the heroes.

But Collie didn't go unnoticed by Marsha
who knew about his love for poetry and wild animals.
And Marsha didn't go unnoticed by Collie
who knew about her soft laughter
and her secret affection for science fiction movies.
And maybe that's why they loved each other so
and why they were so quiet about it, their love.
Because they weren't heroes—
just people, loving.
At Mirabeau B. Lamar everyone's attention was on
which hero liked which hero.
No one really knew about Marsha Cates
and Collie Sims and their love for each other.
No one really cared.

Except perhaps a few in the French horn section.

So when Collie was hit by a drunken driver
one warm spring night on his way home from Marsha's,
where they had talked about arctic foxes
and watched *Close Encounters of the Third Kind*
in the same evening, when Marsha had played that tune,
A-B-G-G-D in perfect whole notes on her French horn,
most people at Mirabeau B. Lamar
couldn't even picture his face
      when they closed their eyes.

But not Marsha who couldn't *not* picture his face.

And weeks, even months later
      most people at Mirabeau B. Lamar
hadn't heard that Marsha still loved Collie
or even that she ever had.
Least of all the glamour crowd.

That didn't matter to Marsha.
She knew Collie didn't care about being
something he wasn't.

But she did know something about Collie and herself,
something shared, something pure
      and sweet and important.
It was just that she couldn't find the way to tell it.

She wanted to—
how important Collie's loving had been,
how that counted.

It drove her day and night
through home room
through band practice

through dinner at night
through her dreams.
But she couldn't find the way.

And only a few people in the French horn section
had the slightest idea that Marsha, so quiet
and unnoticed was coming undone.

So it figured that the French horn section knew first
when Marsha Cates stopped marching
    in the middle of the field
during half-time at the homecoming game.
She just stopped while the band marched around her
and left her there on the 43rd yard line
all alone facing the bleachers and all the heroes.
For a moment no one noticed
for Marsha Cates wasn't the noticed kind.
But then someone pointed to her,
    all alone on the 43rd yard line.
Everyone in that stadium turned
    their faces in her direction
while Marsha Cates shifted from one foot to another,
slowly lifted her French horn to her lips
her body perfectly straight beneath the burning lights.

At first the notes cracked
    like they couldn't find their place.
She stopped for a full minute
    while the crowd in the stands
shifted too. Someone snickered, pointed
but that didn't matter because soon
from out of her rented French horn
a smooth, mellow tune
lifted into the air.

Five perfect notes: A-B-G-G-D
It rang out:
    one syllable for each note
We must not forget.
We must not forget.

As Marsha Cates played,
one by one
the French horn section
joined her on the field
in an arc
golden horns raised
bodies straight, and
played the notes
over and over
and over
until everyone in the stadium
including the heroes
saw faces
in the golden notes
faces loved
faces remembered,
Collie Sims' face
and knew something
so sweet
so pure
so important
that for just
the briefest moment
no one in that stadium was a hero,
least of all Marsha Cates.

They were all just people,
loving

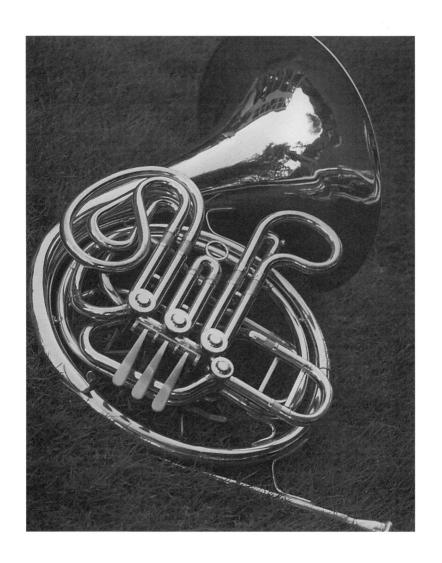

Paper/Pen/Poem:

A Young Writer's Way to Begin

The Big Question

I have never, in all my years of writing and teaching, met a young person who doesn't *want* to write. You may be afraid to write, but even fear doesn't erase the yearning. For it's in us, as human beings, to crave expression, to tell a story, to say something in a new way.

Saying who you are is as basic as breathing and eating, sleeping and playing.

Writing especially helps you create order out of the jumble that makes up your day-to-day life and helps you make sense of the happenings that occur from moment to moment. This includes the small moments as well as the big ones.

It helps you tell how you felt when you saw a hummingbird hover for a split second above your head. It allows you to show how the mountain looked with a ring of clouds around its peak. It gives you an opportunity to explain why it was so important to throw rocks at the Coca-Cola™ cans in the ditch.

I want to tell you a story.

When I was a little over two years old, my mother handed me a box of crayons and stood me in front of our garage wall which was, to my-two-year old sensibilities, a huge canvas, an enormous blank sheet of paper. The crayons and the garage wall were a gift, a place for me to put my earliest scribbles—and that's what they were— scribbles.

For me, the garage wall was a place to begin my journey as a writer. At the age of two, such a huge blank space was thrilling, exhilarating. I could walk along the wall with a fistful of crayons and make a bumpy rainbow of colors. It was a joyful space for color and circles and up-and-down hills and valleys where wild, wild flowers and one-of-a-kind species of birds and rabbits hid among them. Only I could see them peering out from the wall. To anyone else, I'm sure they were only scribbles, but that didn't matter because they made perfect sense to me.

When I learned to write, paper replaced the garage wall. The blank page should have been like it—a wild place to explore with my words and pencil.

Instead, it became a tightly ordered page of blue horizontal lines, penned in by red vertical lines on the margins. Writing had to fit within these lines. It was as if writing became imprisoned by the blue and red bars and gradually faded into the gray figures that my pencil placed there. All color disappeared.

I think this happens to many of us. Our words become prisoners and no longer really belong to us. Rather, they belong to an assignment that we have to complete for a grade.

And so we forget what writing is really for—to help us figure out our own stories. To help us say who we are.

"Oh yeah!" you say, "to tell my stories, that's what writing is for." Remembering this is exhilarating! It sparks something basic in you, something you knew when you were two and knew what to do with a handful of crayons. The old yearning to write emerges and says, "Yes, let's get with it, let's get that pen on the paper. Let's tell the world who I am!"

But then the "Big Question" raises its ugly head like a giant piranha waiting to snap up all those lovely words. The question that stalls more people than any other question in the universe. The question that has prevented thousands, maybe millions of people, from writing: *Where to begin?*

Why is this such a loaded question? Why is it so laden with fear? I believe it's because when we look at our lives, our stories, there's so *much* to tell, that it seems like a huge jumble, an enormous mass of bits and pieces that don't seem to fit in any logical order. The array of possibilities is numbing. It freezes our pencils in mid-air and keeps us from ever making a single mark.

Where to begin? It's so big that it makes writing feel impossible.

I want to tell you something true. *Where to begin?* isn't as big as it's cracked up to be. It's just that there are so many answers, it seems larger than it really is. The key to cracking the question is to break it down into small parts. How?

First of all, you take paper and pen. You give yourself some time and a quiet place. And you begin to look—at objects, at moments, at people, at places, at wishes and dreams—and that's where writing begins.

The aim of this book is to give you opportunities to find the answers to that question through poetry. Why poetry? For one, you can hold it in your hand, you can breathe it in a single breath, you can see the one moment in time that clarifies everything.

Writing begins with the small crystal, the grain of sand that grows and becomes something larger, something like a pearl, something with shape and purpose and meaning.

With each poem in this book, I've written a few sentences about the poem, and then afterwards, I've given you a handful of invitations to write about your own experiences. What you write may take the form of a poem, maybe a song, or it may become something longer and larger—a short story, an essay, or even a novel. Right now, the form doesn't matter. What matters is that you write. What matters is that you set your words loose and let them say who you are. There will be time later for shaping and revising. For now, what matters is that you begin.

Come with me. I'll show you a way . . .

Your Own Writing Book:
The Garage Wall Between Covers

Before you start, give yourself a blank book. It doesn't have to be fancy or expensive. A plain wire-bound notebook will do. Figure out whether you like blank pages or lined pages. What are you most comfortable with? Try both. At first, you might want to start with a small notebook, one that will fit in your pocket or your purse. Or you might like a large sketch pad that takes up your whole lap. Choose what makes you most comfortable. You might prefer writing on a typewriter or a computer. If you do that, be sure to print out your writing and keep it in a loose-leaf binder.

You can call this book a journal, a diary, a "Captain's Log," a notebook, or even give it a title like "Musings" or "Pages for my Thoughts to Be" or "Me on Paper." Be creative. Writers love to make up titles.

On the inside cover write the date. A friend of mine puts a current photo of himself on the inside covers of each of his writing books. He claims it helps him remember "whose stories he's telling." I think it's a wonderful idea. When the book is full, add the finishing date and start a new book.

Remember the garage wall I drew on when I was two? Think of this book as your own garage wall, a place to "scribble" to your heart's abandon.

What you write in it doesn't have to make sense. It doesn't have to be perfect or correct or logical. It only has to be written down. And like my garage wall, it will become a starting point, a departure on your writing journey, a beginning for all the writing that will come later. It's the beginning of *Where to Begin?*

about **A**t the **C**arnival **L**ast **N**ight

I wasn't allowed to go on a real date until I was sixteen. But before that, when I was thirteen or so, I was allowed to go with a group of friends to places like the bowling alley, the skating rink and the Saturday morning matinee at the Broadway Theater. One of our favorite hang-outs was the traveling carnival that set up occasionally at the neighborhood K-Mart store.

Invitations

1. Write about being on a carnival ride—the first time you ever rode a roller coaster, the time the Ferris wheel got stuck, the time you popped three balloons in a row with a dart and won a huge sawdust-filled teddy bear, the time your cotton candy got stuck in your hair.

2. Write about a stolen kiss, such as the one in the poem.

3. Is there a place where you and your friends like to hang out? What makes it a good gathering place? Do you feel safe there? Why or why not? Write about it. Write about something that happened there or might happen there. Write about why it's so special.

4. Who do you like to be with? Write about one of them.

about **Who Would've Thought**

One of my favorite things to do is dance. It always makes me feel lighter. It makes me feel exuberant and joyful even when I've had a bad day. Dancing is a great way to get out of a bad mood, especially when you're in a roomful of other dancers.

Invitations

1. Write the phrase "who would've thought . . ." at the top of your page and make a list of unbelievable incidences that may or may not have occurred. Pick one and keep writing. For example: Who would've thought . . .

. . . my mother would dye her hair bright orange?

. . . a tornado would land right on top of my dresser?

. . . three dollars was enough to buy the dress of my dreams?

. . . I was smart enough to beat my brother at chess?

2. Write about a moment when you were dancing—describe the music, the place, the person or people you were with, the occasion, the time, everything you can remember about it.

3. What might happen if you started dancing in an unusual place—like the school bus, on the moon, in the cafeteria at lunch, in the middle of science class? Write about it.

4. Write about something that happened at a party. Give all the details, starting with the place.

5. Have you ever been to a school dance? Write about what happened during one particular dance. Write about what happened in between dances.

about **Fields**

My grandmother Marge hated being indoors, so she spent most of her time in her small yard, either tending her vegetable garden, watering her flowers, or just sitting on her patio. Whenever my sisters and cousins and I stayed with her, she let us bring all her old blankets and quilts outdoors. We'd spread them out in a large patchwork and then lie down on our backs and wait for the stars to come out. I remember lying there and feeling as if I were spinning through space and time. Even now, all these years later, I love to lie on a quilt in the early evening and watch the stars appear.

Invitations

1. With so many city lights, it's harder and harder now to see the stars. But even in the brightest downtown, if you look carefully, you can see a few twinkling overhead. Write about stars, about searching for them, about counting them, about learning their names.

2. Can you name the constellations? On a winter's night, I'm always happy to spy Orion, the bear hunter. There's something comforting to me about his steady presence. Is there a constellation that you particularly enjoy spotting? Why? Write about it.

3. There is a great deal of mythology surrounding constellations. Make up your own constellation. Create a myth about it. Tie it to your own life. For example, I'll bet that if I looked closely at the stars, I could find a constellation that looked like a patchwork quilt. My myth would be about a girl who misses her grandmother and so the grandmother pieces together the stars and makes a quilt to remind the girl of her ongoing love for her.

4. My grandmother's quilt was more than just a quilt. It

smelled like her; it was made of all her favorite colors and patterns; it made me feel cozy and warm. What objects in your life remind you of someone? Make a list. For example:

Camel cigarettes—Dad
Rocking chair—Uncle Dave
White shoulders perfume—Karen
Tupperware—Aunt Susan
Knitted afghan—Mom

Next, write about the stories connected with them. This could take many pages. Come back to this invitation again and again.

about **T**he **A**irshow, c. 1929

When I was a teenager, I saw a documentary film about wing walkers and barnstormers. Through the years I've thought about them many times, but with my fear of heights, I've never understood them.

Invitations

1. Look through some magazines such as NATIONAL GEOGRAPHIC or LOOK or TRAVEL or any magazine that might have articles about someone who has an incredibly risky job or hobby—mountain climbing, riding bulls, motorcycle racing. Write a story about one of them.
2. Imagine you were a wing walker. Write about what it would be like. Who would be watching you from the tarmac? What would they say?
3. At some point in our lives, each of us has met with disapproval. Write about one of those times. If you could do it all over, what would you do? Would you change something? Would you do it again? What regrets do you have about it? Sorrows? What did you learn from it? Perhaps you could write this as a letter to whomever disapproved—you don't have to send it. Write it to yourself.

about *Tips from my Grandfather*

Often, parents are too busy to teach us the important things in life such as how to make a stone skip across a pond. But grandparents are a different story. My grandfather taught me many things. He died this past spring at the age of 90, but he left behind a thousand lessons.

Invitations

1. Write about one small moment when someone taught you something. Make a poem out of the directions.

2. Find an interesting stone or shell. Study it. How old do you think it is? What do you think it would tell you if it could talk? What has it seen and heard?

3. Think about all the small things that you do from time to time—spinning coins on the tabletop, throwing sticks for the dog, brushing your teeth, washing dishes, mowing the grass, kicking a can, flipping bottle tops. Make a list, then choose one or two to write about. Keep your writing short.

4. Dig out an old photograph of yourself or a relative, not a portrait, but a picture of someone doing something. Tell the story behind the photo, even if you don't know for sure what is going on. Make it up. Guess. Be as wild as you dare.

5. Study the photograph. Can you tell the story behind it?

about **Lunch**

Moving to a new school changes everything. Divorce changes everything. Death of a loved one changes everything. While change often brings a chance to start all over, it's not always easy.

Invitations

1. Write about someone who has recently come into your life.

2. Write about someone who has recently moved away from your life.

3. Write about lunch time at your school. Write about one particular incident at lunch.

4. What if your lunch bag held wishes? What would they be?

5. Write about the new kid in your class. What is it you like about him or her? What is it you dislike? Have you ever been in that kid's shoes? What was the hardest thing about being the new kid? What makes a new friendship possible? Write about it?

about **S**wifts

My husband's family owns a ranch in La Grange, Texas. On the back porch is the most wonderful swing in the world. I like to wake up early, take my journal out there and write. The swifts, who make their nests in the porch beams, aren't always happy to see me.

Invitations

1. Do you have a special place where you can just be quiet? A place to take your journal and jot down your thoughts? Write about it. Describe it. Draw it.

2. In the hustle and bustle of our everyday lives, we sometimes forget to notice things like spider webs and kittens. Make a list of everyday things that don't seem very significant because they're so common. Write a poem about them. Maybe your list will turn into a poem.

3. Imagine that you are a bird or some animal. Write an account of your day. What would you have for breakfast? How would you spend your morning, afternoon and evening? What would be important to you?

4. What if you were sitting on the porch in the picture— who would you like to have next to you? What would you like that person to know? What would you like to know about him or her?

about **Emergence**

Before I was old enough to drive, I used to love to sit in my father's car, especially when it was raining because the rain seemed to separate me from the rest of the world. I was safe and dry in the front seat of the car. Sometimes I took a book out there to read, sometimes I practiced my flute, sometimes I wrote in my journal. I used to pretend that the car was my own magic carpet and would take me wherever I wanted to go.

Invitations

1. If you had a magic carpet, where would you go? Would it be someplace you've never been before? Someplace exotic or far away? Or, would it be someplace familiar, like your grandparents' house or a friend's. Why would you go there?

2. Get out a map. Make a list of cities that are named after animals. Make a list of places that are named after flowers. Trees. Objects. Tribes. People. Pick one and make up a story about why that place was so named. Do it again with another place.

3. If you had your own town, what would you name it? Why? Make up your own rules about living there.

about **Mutual Attraction**

I confess: I'm a cat lover. There aren't too many spaces in my personal history when there wasn't a cat or two. I love the mystery of them.

Invitations

1. Write about a particular pet that you've lived with.

2. If that pet could "worship" something, what might it be—the food dish? The front porch? The catnip mouse? The barn? Write about it.

3. Write a story from the cat's point of view—or a gerbil's point of view, a horse's, a dog's, a rat's. Choose an animal and tell a tale from their viewpoint.

about **A Pillow Case**

Saturdays are good for sleeping late, aren't they?

Invitations

1. Keep a notebook or journal beside your bed. As soon as you wake up in the morning, write down any dream or dreams that you can recall. Don't try to figure them out, just write them down.

2. What dreams, goals, or wishes do you have? Make a list. Keep adding to it.

about **S**ide *by* **S**ide

On the last day of 1995 I attended a grave side funeral at the Washington Cemetery in Houston. The day was cold and wet—it matched the way I felt. Then, as I was driving away, I saw the two headless angels, perfectly still, and yet almost poised for flight. The sight was so startling that it stayed with me long after I left.

Invitations

1. Study the picture. What do you think happened to the angels' heads? If the angels could talk, what do you think they would tell?

2. Write about a funeral you've attended. Just make lists of everything you can think of about that funeral—the place where it was held, the cemetery, the people who attended, remarks made, what people wore, food served afterwards, how long it took, the season it was, newspaper clippings, things you remember most, the different feelings you felt. Then go back and write a poem or paragraph about one of those things. Write many poems and paragraphs until you've used up all the lists.

3. Write about a time you were lost.

about The Swimmer

A selkie, according to legend, is a seal who turns into a woman when captured by a fisherman. She marries him and has a family, but can never give up her longing for her watery home. However, if she returns to the sea, she will have to abandon her earth-family forever. I've never been a competitive swimmer, but I have had the experience of swimming hard, through cramps and pain, until I didn't feel them at all. I can recall once when it seemed like I was actually part of the water around me.

Invitations

1. Write about a time when you had to push through something. It could be a time when you felt like giving up, or you felt like you'd hit a dead end. What kept you going? How did it turn out?

2. Choose a mythological character, like a selkie, and write a story about her or him that takes place now, in modern times.

3. What are your favorite sports? Do you participate in one or more? Write about what it's like to be a football player, a tennis player, a soccer or baseball player, a swimmer. What is it about that sport that makes you love it and sometimes hate it? Why do you keep playing?

4. Write about one small moment when you were participating in a game and something significant happened. Try to get down to the very essence of that moment. Write it in one paragraph. Write it in one sentence. Write it in four words or less.

about *Giving* **Up**

Some things are so hard to give up, especially first things like bicycles and bunk beds and bracelets, even though we know we've outgrown them. Some things, like my bike, turn out to be wiser than we are.

Invitations

1. Have you ever had to give up something you've outgrown? What was it? Did you give it up gladly? Were you forced to give it up? Did something take its place? Write a good-bye letter to the object you gave up.

2. Have you ever known someone who owned something that you really wanted? A new bike? A toy? A guitar? A great pair of jeans? Write about the person and the object. Tell about how you felt about them—the person and the object.

3. Have you ever had to learn a hard lesson? Did you come to "see" something in a different way? Write about that. Call it "My Hard Lesson."

about *The Pebble*

Have you ever watched a very small child at play? Everything is of equal value. A pebble has just as much worth as a diamond; a plastic bowl is just as important as an expensive toy. Here's the thing: an oyster makes a pearl from a grain of sand. A poet makes a poem from a bowl of words.

Invitations

1. Take a daily newspaper or an old magazine. Cut out several words and lay them out on the table, then shuffle them around until you've made a poem. Paste it in your notebook. Do it again.

2. Put a pebble in your pocket to remind you about small things.

3. Start a collection of pebbles, feathers, twigs. Study them. What would they tell you if they could talk? Take notes.

about *Javier*

One of the best things about going to Pearl Rucker Elementary was the library. The librarian there quickly found out how much I loved horses so each week she set aside a book about them just for me. Later, when I was in junior high, I had to ride the city bus to get to school. My bus always arrived about an hour before the bell rang. On cold mornings, the school librarian would sometimes take pity on me and the other early birds and let us into the warm library. I wish I could remember those librarians' names, for I owe them a tremendous debt of gratitude.

Invitations

1. Write about a teacher, a librarian, a coach, a mentor, a counselor, a parent or grandparent, anyone who has made a difference in your life. Write about one small moment that you spent with that person. Make a list of all the things that make the person special. Write a letter to them telling them all the ways they're important to you. Send it.

2. Write a "letter poem"—start it with, *Dear Special Person/Remember the time . . . .*

3. Make a list of all your favorite books, including the ones you loved when you were very young. Which is your very favorite? Write about it. Write about the experience of reading it—did someone read it to you? Did you read it out loud? Did you read it all alone? Did it change the way you looked at life? How? Write about it.

about **T**hat **K**iss

The first time I was ever kissed by a boy was on the stairway at school. I don't think he intended to kiss me. He just did. His name was Mike Harrison. What a sweet moment, what a sweet boy.

Invitations

1. Write about your first kiss. Make it into a poem.

2. All kinds of moments occur "in between" things—in between classes, in between meals, in between shows on the television, in between the innings of a ball game, in between the car and the back door, in between letters, in between dances. Write about some "in between" moments.

3. Sometimes things happen that make us feel like we're flying or floating, as if our feet have lifted right off the ground. Write about a time when that happened to you. Something that made you feel so good the ground seemed to disappear.

About *Tropism*

It seemed to me that every single year in science class, we studied tropism and phototropism.

Invitations

1. Write poems about science projects.

2. Think of scientific terms—hypotheses, organic, pre-historic, osmosis, germination, Coriolis force. Make a list of them as possible titles of poems. Choose one. Write it at the top of the page. Begin the poem with the words, "You need:" then write on. Try the same thing with mathematical words—Celsius, circumference, kilometer, Richter scale, square inch, trillion. Try again with inventions and inventors--talking machines, moving pictures, seaplanes, cameras, vending machines.

3. Create a title for a "homework machine." Write a poem that explains how it guarantees straight A's.

about **Keeping His Head**
For Jacob

These days we don't give ourselves many opportunities to gaze off into space. My oldest son Jacob is a great daydreamer. He comes by it honestly, since both his mother and father are daydreamers too.

Invitations

1. Wouldn't it be great if we could have a "daydream" class right along with English and Math? If you could, what would you daydream about? Do you think you'd get bored? What other classes would you like to have? Maybe storytelling? How about an "imagination class"? A "creativity class." Make a list. Then make up the class rules and requirements.

2. Make a list of your favorite daydreams. Write about them.

3. Take some time to watch the clouds. What shapes do they take on? Do you think angels live there? Draw a picture of clouds.

4. If you could dye your hair a different color, what would it be? Why would you choose that color? What is your favorite color, anyway? Why?

about **S**acred **B**ear of **H**okkaido

On the Japanese island of Hokkaido, the brown bear, *higuma*, is sacred. Every spring a cub is captured by the Ainu people. The women of the village care for it all summer. Then in the fall, the bear is killed so that it can become a messenger to the bear god who lives in the mountain temple. If the Ainu have taken good care of the cub, it will deliver the message that the bear was revered and loved as much as one of the children. This will insure a good crop and plentiful fishing.

Invitations

1. This poem is call a haiku. It's an ancient form of poetry from Japan. The idea of a haiku is to create one or more pictures on paper with as few words as possible. Why not write a daily haiku?

2. Think of something incredibly big—a bear, an oil well, a mountain, a skyscraper—and write a poem about it in three lines or less. Ten words or less. Five syllables or less.

3. Take a folktale or a legend and condense it into a poem.

about *The Inner Ear*

This is a list poem. One of the things I love to do with poetry is to play with words and sounds. In this instance, I made a list of all the ways in which I could honor my ears. In addition there is an inner ear hidden on each line. Can you find it?

Invitations

1. Make a list of short words, such as ear, it, at, eat, air, and hide them inside longer words. Connect the words and write a poem.

2. Write down your favorite 100 words. Write several poems using these words.

3. Write down your next favorite 100 words. Write more poems.

4. Make a list of words that only begin with a certain letter, say, "s," and make poems using those words only.

5. Play!

about *Where the Colors Slip Through*

One morning, when I was perhaps fifteen, I slipped out of our house where my father and stepmother and both my sisters were still sleeping, and went for an early-morning ride all alone. The new hours of the morning, before the day awakened, were peaceful and enchanting at the same time. While I rode along, atop my gentle horse, I felt very aware of the natural world around me, as if all my senses had been fine-tuned.

Invitations

1. Get into the habit of taking walks, of finding a place to be that's not indoors. What do you see? What do you hear? What do you smell? Write about all these. Take your notebook with you when you go and jot down quick notes.

2. Make an appointment to watch the sun rise. Get up early and step outside. Write about what the sunrise looks like in as few words as possible. Try a haiku—a three line poem that is designed to express one single moment. Write lots of sunrise haiku. Try sunset haiku.

3. Make a list of all the things that are welcome in your life. What are the things you embrace? What are the things you're grateful for? Make a list and keep adding to it. Start a new list every day.

about *Just People*

After I wrote this poem, I realized that I had written it for
a friend of mine whose son was killed by a drunken driver.
He was also a French horn player. So many times, writing
has helped me deal with difficult moments. It is also a way
of honoring people who are important to us.

Invitations

1. Do you play a musical instrument? Write a poem
called, "learning to play the . . . piano, violin, whatever ."
Write about what it's like to play that instrument. Do you
have a friend who plays? Write about that friend.

2. Are you a member of a club? A band? An orchestra?
A team? Write about the people that make up that particular group. Maybe you have a circle of friends that are very
close. Write about them.

3. When you write, you don't have to write about the
way something really happened. You can write about the
way you wished it had happened. Fiction is the only place
we get to grant wishes. Grant one on the page.

4. Is there someone you really miss? Write about him or
her.